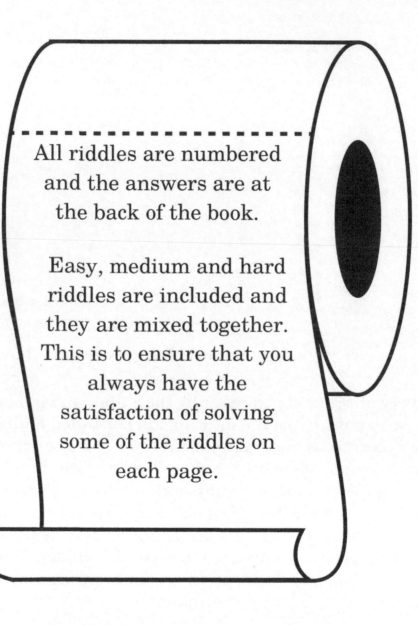

All riddles are numbered
and the answers are at
the back of the book.

Easy, medium and hard
riddles are included and
they are mixed together.
This is to ensure that you
always have the
satisfaction of solving
some of the riddles on
each page.

Hello! Have you forgotten your phone?

Never fear as this book is dedicated to everyone who loves to spend time in the bathroom.

Puzzle over fiendish riddles as nature takes its course and never be bored in the bathroom again!

1. You hold me with two hands but I don't return the favour
   The action's in your grasp but on screen you see the labour
   I have many buttons that you press in combination
   I am no conductor but I do work at a station

2. My name is John
   I'm often white
   If you're desperate
   I'm a welcome sight
   I'm often engaged
   But never Wed
   You use me more often
   Than your own bed

3. I'm tasty and hot
   Can be in a pickle
   I don't cost a lot
   But more than a nickel
   You can pick me up
   When out in a car
   I disappear faster
   Than a shooting star

4. I have a face but cannot talk
   I have a tail but no legs to walk
   Everyone likes to keep me at home
   But they take me out whenever they roam

5. In a one story house, everything is painted blue.
   The walls are painted blue.
   The doors are painted blue.
   The floors are painted blue.
   The ceilings are painted blue.
   What color are the stairs painted?

6. What is incredibly easy to get into and very difficult to get out of?

7. What word contains 26 letters yet consists of only 3 syllables?

8. A man went out to walk his dog and whilst he was out, it started to rain. His dog got very wet. The man had not got an umbrella so his coat became soaking wet and his shoes were sodden however not a hair on his head got wet - why?

9. I'm tasty to eat but before you can do so, you have to open me. However I don't have a lid and you can't tear me open. How do you get me open?

10. Which month of the year has 28 days?

11. I'm small and round and have a tail,
    I move from side to side
    I have a trusty arrow,
    but no bow was supplied
    Hold me as you go explore
    I'll take you all around
    But please don't put me on my back,
    I'm useless upside down
    What am I?

12. I'm 3 letters
    Remove one and I become stronger
    Remove two and I become 10
    What am I?

13. What does nobody want yet also nobody wants to loose this once they have it?

14. You want this coat to be wet when you put it on. What kind of coat is it?

15. What is it that you own and belongs to you yet other people use it more than you do yourself?

16. Before the Nile was discovered, what was the longest river in the world?

17. What always goes up but never comes back down?

18. What goes further when it goes more slowly?

19. Some of us will swing, though others like to slide.
    We stand with every building though not out or inside.
    We shake hands when we meet, or I simply give a glance.
    Until a hole appears before your very stance.
    What am I?

20. Contrary to my name, I am no Queen
    Hold things against me and my measure is seen
    What am I?

21. Remove the head that sits on top of me
    An increase in my height is plain to see
    What am I?

22. The person who makes me says nothing
    The person who takes me knows nothing
    The person who knows me wants to get rid of me
    What am I?

23. What breaks yet never falls and what falls but never breaks?

24. Where is there is no North, West nor East and the weather is not fit for man or beast?

25. A king, a queen and twins all lay in a large room yet there are no people anywhere to be seen.
    How is this true?

26. I am an odd number. Remove one letter and I am now even. What number am I?

27. Which month of the year is the month where people get the least sleep?

28. What has an eye but cannot spy?

29. Made of metal, I've endured a hit
    Now in the corner I have to sit
    My primary aim is to grip a tree
    By changing from a C to a B
    What am I?

30. Stronger than steel though not man made
    Hidden in darkness - I prefer the shade!
    Sticky with glue, catching those I find
    Yet no-one wants me - I'm much maligned
    What am I?

31. What is so delicate and fragile that saying its name out loud causes it to break?

32. In just one second I fill a room
    Yet no space do I consume
    What am I?

33. Be cruel to me and I'll probably crack
    Smile at me and I'll always smile back
    What am I?

34. A person crosses a river without using a bridge or a boat and still does not get wet.
    How?

35. What type of rocks are never found on a river bed?

36. When you sing, I come alive but shortly afterwards, I die.
    When I die you, you clap and cheer, but I'll be back again next year.
    What am I?

37. If I work too hard, I'll cool off with a fan
    I'll take you to a spider's home or into a trash can
    Though they say I'm heartless, you use me for my brain
    I can catch a nasty bug and never feel pain
    What am I?

38. How many days can a person go without sleeping?

39. A person is sitting in a house reading a book.
    It is dark outside and inside the house there are no lights on, nor candles.
    How is the person reading the book?

40. All over the world, people come to see me.
    Each person spends several years with me.
    If you are too young, you cannot visit me.
    If you are too old, you can't come either unless it is
    required as part of your job.
    I can make you smarter and wealthier.
    What am I?

41. I have five sides but when you close me, only four.
    I travel far and wide but you find me on the floor.
    What am I?

42. I part the waves and line up the strands
    An unveiling tool in the user's hands.
    What am I?

43. There were two sailors on a ship.
    One was looking North and
    One was looking South.
    Yet they could both see each other.
    How is this possible?

44. A mother has two sons. They were both born on the
    same day, in the same month, in the same year but
    they are not twins.
    How can this be?

45. What sweet 5 letter word has only one left when two
    letters are removed?

46. People pay me to fill holes with silver or gold.
    What am I?

47. I fly through an open door
    Enjoy the sweetest drink galore
    Carry my cargo back to my mates
    Dance to explain where the gold awaits
    What am I?

48. I like to travel in a bunch
    Shed my coat, you can take a munch
    Whole or split, I'm on the table
    From green to yellow I am able
    What am I?

49. I'm bound to the ground and cannot run
    On a unclouded day, I face the sun
    I can pierce you until you bleed
    Yet you gift my beauty to friends in need
    What am I?

50. I am white, my twin is black
    We stand cheek by jowl
    Upside down I bring forth snow
    But too much makes things foul
    What am I?

51. You grab me by my ear
    And press your lips to me
    Up and down I move
    Like a boat on a choppy sea
    Hot and dark to look at
    I'm known throughout the earth
    Grasp me in your hand
    My scent and taste gives me worth
    What am I?

52. I have two banks but no money
    What am I?

53. Never dropped but often broken
    Free to give, a friendship token
    What am I?

54. A person goes into a coffee shops and they ask the
    barista if he can help him by giving a glass of water.
    Instead, the barista pulls out a gun and points it at
    the other person. The person thanks the barista and
    leaves.
    Why?

55. You're always quick to answer me
    But I don't ask you any questions
    What am I?

56. Inside a locked room, a person lies on the floor.
    They are injured and there is a pool of water at the
    side of them.
    No-one else is in the room.
    What caused this person's injuries?

57. I weigh next to nothing yet you would not be able to
    hold me for more than 5 minutes.
    What am I?

58. Sharp enough to cut, yet you hold me to your throat
    When I'm at work, through the snow I float
    Bristly when I begin, smooth when I depart
    Use me skillfully and I'll keep you looking smart
    What am I?

59. A person wearing a backpack is lying face down in a field of corn.
The sun is shining and a small plane is flying overhead.
The person is dead but how did they die?

60. It's 2am.
A person staying in a hotel room is wide awake.
They make a phone call but say nothing.
Now they can get to sleep and all is well.
Who did they call?

61. Sometimes I'm smelly and dirty but everyone wants me.
What am I?

62. I have no mouth yet I can speak and cheer
I have no ears but I can always hear
I lurk in tunnels, hollows and caves
I return to you like a beach shore wave
What am I?

63. A person sits down to eat in a restaurant and orders soup.
As they are about to eat, they spot a small fly floating on the surface of the soup.
They call the waiter and ask for the soup to be replaced.
However, when the soup comes back, the diner can tell it is the original bowl of soup with the fly removed.
How can they tell it is not fresh soup?

64. What do you call two ants who are from Italy?

65. I am a box with no lock but many keys
I can touch your soul with gentle ease
From a humble room to a cavernous hall
In the right hands, you'll be in my thrall
What am I?

66. At night, you see them reawaken
By day, they vanish, without being taken
What am they?

67. A prisoner is held in a cell.
The cell has thick walls and a thick steel door.
The cell has no water nor water supply.
Outside the cell in the corridor there is a drinking water fountain.
How does the prisoner get a drink of water without help?

68. What kind of animals can jump higher than a car?

69. At 4pm in the afternoon, a person is standing in the middle of a field.
There are no trees in the field.
There is not a cloud in the sky.
However, the person does not have a shadow.
Why do they have no shadow?

70. In a market, shop or trading place
You confirm the asking price
Take away just my front
I become human avarice.
What am I?

71. Water is the reason I am here
    But add me to water, and I disappear!
    What am I?

72. A top scientist had a brother who was a renowned
    artist but what relation was the scientist to the
    artist? Clue: 'brother' is a wrong answer

73. John, Alex, James and Lisa all live in the same
    house.
    John and Alex go out to see a movie.
    When they get home, Lisa is lying in a pool of water
    on the floor and is dead.
    No-one calls the police.
    James has killed her but he receives no punishment.
    Why does he go unpunished?

74. What occurs four times in a teenager's life, once in
    your adult lifespan and never in your childhood?

75. I've known you well now for a while
    I never fail to make you smile
    You pick me up both night and day
    Apply a paste then rub it away
    Round and round, up and down
    Plunge into water. I almost drown!
    What am I?

76. I'm not a ship but I do have sails
    I'm happy in a fearsome gale
    Never at sea, always on the ground
    Slowly working away with little sound.
    What am I?

77. What has lots of diamonds but only has minimal worth?

78. People need me and want to keep me but they are always giving me to someone else.
What am I?

79. In his own home, a person watches whilst a robbery takes place yet they do not respond and they do absolutely nothing.
Why?

80. A motorist accidentally drives over some broken glass in the road.
They are able to travel another 50 miles even though one of the tires is punctured.
How is this possible?

81. A person falls off a 25ft ladder but they are completely unhurt.
How is this possible?

82. You belong to me for hours each day
I tell you stories whilst you're away
You catch me by night - by day I am gone
If you miss me too much, your suffering's begun
What am I?

83. You spy me where I cannot actually be
I pop up at whim - you can't fail to see me
What am I?

84. In Winter months I bare my soul
    With Summer, I don my green stole
    Between these times a golden hue
    Until the wind viciously blew
    What am I?

85. What is found in the middle of water but is not a
    ship?

86. When outside taking exercise, I received this
    unwanted item although I had to stop and search for
    it. When I found it, I threw it away.
    What was the item?

87. You see right through me, don't notice I am there
    On a sunny day, I'm known to cast a glare.
    What am I?

88. Effective at cleaning despite its small size
    Twice daily use is advice very wise
    What is it?

89. I come in many varieties of style
    I cannot be smelt, touched or tasted
    I can get you up and moving about
    What am I?

90. Get me wet - it's not a big deal
    Though too much sun does not appeal
    If knocked, my color may quickly change
    Although I come in quite a range
    Look after me, give me some care
    You only have one, there is no spare.
    What am I?

91. Hand-like to look at but cannot hold
You need me most when outside is cold
What am I?

92. Oh! to receive such a thing
It gives your soul a little 'zing'
To get one can bring maximum joy
Whether you're a girl or boy
It's message can be so sincere
And sometimes cause a little tear
What is this?

93. A person leaves home and drives to a 24hr shop
They get what they want and drive back
When they arrive home, it's is 5 minutes earlier
than when they left.
How is this possible?

94. This sentance conntains two misstakes.
How many mistakes are there in the previous
sentence?

95. It's lessons should be heeded
As they are often needed
Impossible to change but can be repeated
Facts, events, places, even Kings unseated.
What am I?

96. My story can be a tome of grief
Your help is required to turn a new leaf.
Stiff is my spine and sometimes I crack
But entertaining with tales is my knack
What am I?

97. I do not speak and cannot hear
But will tell the truth when you are near
What am I?

98. What has a slender neck but no head?

99. What has no hands but might come knocking and if it does, it will benefit you to receive it?

100. Monochrome, no color to see
Stuck at the base yet moves fluidly
Out with the sun, gone with the rain
Emotionless and feeling no pain
What am I?

101. John Wrong went on trial 8 times last week. Each time he was accused of the murder of Susan Smith. Each time he was found guilty of the murder. How is this possible?

102. A horse jumps over a tower and lands on a bishop who then disappears.
What has happened?

103. Round and round a circle, a uniform pie chart
Filled with decoration, a unique work of art
Your thoughtless interference tears me apart
A filling for the hole that was there at the start
What is being described?

104. A man watches as his wife emerges from a burning house. She runs towards him with her clothes in flames yet he is not worried about her. She is perfectly fine.
How is this possible?

105. A person has just had a hospital appointment and is making their way home. On the way, they hear a phone ringing. They are very excited and race home to give their family the great news!
What was the news?

106. I can be driven but I have no wheels
I can be sliced but I stay in one piece
I can be chipped but not eaten
What am I?

107. Once given one, you'll have either two or none?
What is it?

108. I am freezing cold yet I never wear a coat.
What am I?

109. Tom's parents have three sons. They are called Snap, Crackle and ??
What is the name of the third son?

110. What is full of holes yet it can hold a lot of water?

111. What lies in front of you but is impossible for you to see?

112. If two's company and three's a crowd, what are four and five?

113. When you need me, you throw me away.
When you no longer need me, you get me back.
What am I?

114. What moves without you often noticing and cries but has no eyes?

115. What comes down but never goes up?

116. Round like a wheel, deep like a cup
Yet a powerful tow truck cannot pull it up?
What is it?

117. What question is it impossible to answer 'Yes' to?

118. Two people take part in a parachute jump. They
drift off course and land away from the intended
drop zone. They start to walk. One walks North and
one walks South. After 30 minutes walking, they
meet up.
How is this possible?

119. A person is standing in the living room of a house.
There is no-one else in the house. Suddenly, the
person puts their hands in the air. Next, they laugh
and let their hands drop. They exit the building.
Can you explain this?

120. I'm often running although legs I have none.
You need me but I don't need anyone.
What am I?

121. What is seen in the middle of March and April that
can't be seen at the beginning or end of either of
those months?

122. The first time I lie
Is when I die
What am I?

123. When you loose something, why is it always in the
very last place that you look?

124. I have many keys but no locks,
I have space but I'm not a room,
I have a home but no possessions
You can enter but it's impossible to go inside
What am I?

125. I can't touch but you can hold me
Always wet but never moldy
Often bites but seldom nips
To use me well you must own wits.
What am I?

126. I have a head but no mouth to talk
Four legs, but cannot run or walk
Just one foot and I'm used at night
Never to be found on a campsite
What am I?

127. I have golden brown hair and I clean up after you.
What am I?

128. A person is on an airplane when a fire breaks out.
They panic and decide to open the emergency door
and throw themselves out of the plane. Although
they are not wearing a parachute, they are
uninjured and survive their exit from the plane.
How is this possible?

129. What can an elephant make that no other animal
can make?

130. Same word - different spelling - what word is this?
You can smell me
You can spend me
You can deliver me

131. I'm black when you get me, ready to cook
Red when you use me, just take a look
White at my end, to the rubbish I'm took
What am I?

132. I have rings but not of gold
Another each year as I grow old
What am I?

133. Made of carbon inside a tree
Use me wisely and words you'll see
Push me around, give me a press
As I move about, I become less
What am I?

134. My underside smooth but my back full of grip
As part of a trick, I'm known to flip
What am I?

135. With a sharp knife, you cut me deep
Then can't help but have a little weep
What am I?

136. Stronger than steel
Weighs more than a ton
Easy to make and
Scared of the sun
What am I?

137. If one person has me, then I am a burden
If two people have me, I am priceless
Yet I cannot be bought
What am I?

138. When I'm born, I swirl and fly
For most of my life, I tend to lie
When dead, I just run on by
What am I?

139. When I'm alive, you bury me in the soil
When I'm dead, you dig me up
What am I?

140. You give me to someone else yet you also keep me
What am I?

141. What has one eye yet cannot see a single thing?

142. Name something so easy to make that even children
can make it yet it is invisible and no-one can see it.

143. What has a bottom at the top?

144. Name three consecutive days where none of them
are from the list Monday, Tuesday, Friday or
Sunday.

145. On the outside, I am green.
On the inside, I am white.
Inside the white, I am red.
Inside the red, I have lots of babies.
What am I?

146. You buy me so that you can eat
Yet I am never consumed.
What am I?

147. I have many sisters yet I am an only child.
Can you explain this?

148. I sit above you but never judge
I protect you and keep you warm
What am I?

149. I never touch you, yet I can heal you.
What am I?

150. A hammer and anvil, precious like jewels
Yet you can never touch these tools
What am I?

151. Penguins are not frightened of polar bears
Why is this?

152. When you divide this number by itself, the answer is
NOT 1
What is the number?

153. Alex had his birthday yesterday and was 17 years
old.
This year, Alex will celebrate his 18th birthday.
What date is Alex's birthday?

154. You cannot touch me but you can change me.
You use me every day but you never see me.
What am I?

155. Max and Mim are twins and were born 10 minutes
apart.
Max is the eldest and has enjoyed 20 birthdays.
However, Mim has only had 5 birthdays.
Can you explain this?

156. A rich celebrity lives in a large house in London and has staff to look after their every need.

One of the members of staff has stolen an expensive watch and the police are called.

All the staff have alibis but the police know one of them is lying and arrest this person.

The cook was making Christmas dinner.

The maid was tidying the bedroom

The gardener was cutting the grass in the garden.

The butler was polishing some silverware.

Which member of staff was lying?

157. The following dates all have something in common

March 3

November 8

September 9

October 7

What links the dates?

158. To join two things, I'm just the trick

Strong to hold and firm to stick

Touch my surface, have a feel

Not at all sticky where I seal

What am I?

159. Imagine you are in a room.

The door is locked and there are no windows

It is pitch black inside the room and you cannot see a thing.

How do you escape from the room?

160. What goes from Z to A?

161. I can bring you to tears, speed you up, slow you down and, if I am strong enough, even knock you over.
     What am I?

162. I have horses, a cat and even a trunk
     What am I?

163. When does 9 + 5 = 2 ?

164. What tasty, sweet treat has no beginning, middle or end?

165. You can take me if you wish
     You can give me unless you're proud
     I have the ability to change everything
     Yet I cost nothing
     What am I?

166. A person is shot several times by a professional yet they sustain no injuries.
     Can you explain this?

167. If you take more away, I get bigger
     What am I?

168. It takes 5 minutes to boil 1 egg.
     How long does it take to boil 3 eggs?

169. If the Earth has a Heart,
     What does Mars have?

170. I know an artist who drew a flame and drew acclaim and in this riddle, I've told you his name.
     What is his name?

171. What two words, that go together, contain the most letters?

172. I'll give a wave to every guy
But never ever say goodbye
What am I?

173. I am a word of 2 letters and male
Add another letter and I change to a female
Add one more and I become a great person
My whole defines a fantastic woman
What word am I?

174. What makes you young?

175. I am a seven letter word and you would struggle to lift me up.
Remove 1 letters and you will make 80
Remove 1 more letter and you will make 8
What word am I?

176. Take 3/7th of a chicken, 2/3rds of a cat and add 1/2 of a goat.
Where are you now?

177. You are driving a bus.
At the first stop, a family of four get on.
At the second stop, a man and woman get on.
At the third stop, a woman and child get on and a man gets off.
At the fourth stop, two women get on and one woman gets off.
What is the bus driver wearing?

178. You see a car with 4 passengers yet no single person is driving the car even though it is not a driverless car.
Can you explain this.

179. You throw a ball as hard as you can.
The ball does not bounce nor does it hit anything else.
The ball returns to you.
How is this possible?

180. I never ask you a question yet you often feel compelled to answer me.
What am I?

181. I never catch but people like to throw things in my way
I sit up high and watch as people run around all day
When things escape right through my net there's cheering all around
Just for it to fall back through me onto the hard ground
What am I?

182. A dead man is discovered in a locked office.
He is the only person in the room.
He did not commit suicide.
There are no weapons in the room.
The only clue is a sealed envelope on the desk in front of him.
How did he die?

183. I'm small like a mouse
I guard your house
What am I?

184. Chop me in half and I am nothing
Turn me on my side and I am everything
What am I?

185. Add a mathematical symbol to make the number
below equal to seven hundred
7 7 7 7 7

186. Every night, you set me a task yet you seem cross
when I complete the task the following morning.
What am I?

187. I have 6 eggs.
I break 2 of them.
I eat 2 of them.
How many eggs do I have left?

188. Following a tip off, the cops burst into a house to
arrest a man called John.
Inside the house they find a group of 6 people having
dinner.
Without questioning them, they know immediately
which one of them to arrest.
Can you explain why?

189. Mary has quite a few pets.
All except 2 are cats
All except 2 are dogs
All except 2 are rabbits
How many pets does Mary have?

190. A person moves to a new town to live and they have toothache and require a dentist.

There are only two dentists in the town.

The first has a smart looking surgery and excellent teeth.

The second has a scruffy looking surgery and bad teeth.

Which dentist should the person pick and why?

191. I am a 6 letter word and indicate safety and security.

Remove one letter and I become an item of furniture.

Remove one more letter and I am the partner of ready.

Add back the letters you removed and I also become a sanctuary for animals.

What word am I?

192. A grandmother, two mothers and 2 daughters went to a coffee shop. They ordered 1 cup of coffee each. What is the minimum number of coffees they could have ordered?

193. Two friends, Tom and Jim, decide to play a game. Tom tells Jim that he will write Jim's exact weight on a piece of paper and if he does so, Tom will win. However if he does not write Jim's exact weight, then Jim will win.

They do not have any scales so Tom cannot check what Jim weighs and Jim could say anything.

How does Tom win the game?

194. A person is doing their job when their uniform gets a hole torn in it. Shortly afterwards, they die as a result.
Can you explain this?

195. What five letter word becomes two letters which have the same meaning when one is removed?

196. Who is your mother's brother's brother-in-law?

197. As a punishment, a prisoner was made to carry a heavy sandbag across the prison yard and back again every day for a month.
On day 3, they realized they could put something into the bag which would make their task easier as the days went on.
What did they put in the bag?

198. Two policemen see a bus driver travelling the wrong way down a one way street.
Why do they decide to do nothing about this?

199. What goes around the outside of your house, and goes inside your house yet you cannot prevent this from happening?

200. My body large, my head is small, my neck is very long
And when you stroke me, I'll reply, by singing you a song
I am a great companion, you can carry me around
The one thing that I'm known for is my captivating sound
What am I?

201. What would you say I if told you there was a mistake in this sentence? Do you know what the mistake is?

202. This house cannot be bought or sold
Thousands come here to store their gold
Treasure guarded by many sharp darts
Nature's golden bounty in hexagonal carts
What is this?

203. You are a passenger on a train
In front of you is a horse
Behind you is a car
Where are you?

204. Drop me from a height and I'll fly
Drop me into water and watch me slowly die
What am I?

205. I have hands but I cannot offer a greeting
Nor can I give you 5 for I have no fingers
What am I?

206. A young monkey and an old monkey are climbing a coconut tree.
Which monkey gets to the banana first?

207. There are 5 children in a room and no adults. The children are playing quietly.
Susan is drawing a picture.
James is reading a book.
Lucy is playing chess.
Ben is playing with a toy car.
What is Alex doing?

208. There is a family gathering of people who are:
A 5 year old girl
A pregnant lady aged 26
A young man aged 21
Another lady aged 43
A man aged 51
Who is the youngest person present?

209. Own lea too words our rite inn this sentance.
Witch too our write?

210. Which English word has three consecutive double letters?

211. A man is found murdered in his office.
There is a piece of paper on the desk and the dying victim has scrawled the numbers 9, 4, 3 in blood.
The suspects are called Abe, Don, Jim, Sam, Tom.
Which one of them is the culprit?

212. Which number between 1 and 100 has the most syllables when written as a word?

213. A prisoner is trapped in a small room.
The room has 2 doors.
The first door leads to a room that has magnifying glasses as walls so that the sun instantly obliterates anything in the room.
The second door leads to a room where the whole floor is a bottomless pit.
How does the prisoner escape?

214. I float in the breeze
     Lighter than air
     But you could not lift me
     I'm a fragile affair
     What am I?

215. Two fathers and two sons went fishing.
     Each caught a fish but they caught only three fish in
     all.
     Can you explain this?

216. What insect is ¼ Bear and ½ Deer?

217. What mathematical symbol can be placed between
     5 and 7
     so that the result is greater than 5
     and smaller than 7?

218. A woman is sitting in a hotel room.
     A man knocks on the door of the room.
     The woman answers the door.
     The man looks at her then says 'Oh, sorry, I thought
     that this was my room'
     The woman closes the door and calls security.
     What has made her suspicious?

219. A doctor, a lawyer and a teacher all claim that John
     is their brother.
     John says he does not have any brothers.
     Who is not telling the truth?

220. In a line, spaced narrow, not wide
Two long rows, side by side
Pull on me to decide
If we stand together or divide.
What am I?

221. Lucy tells her friend that she can sing lots of songs
with people's names in the lyrics.
The friend has an unusual name, Bartholomew, and
challenges Lucy to sing a song where his name is
part of the lyrics.
Lucy does so immediately.
What song does she sing?

222. You are on your way to visit a friend and have made
some cupcakes to take as a gift.
Between your home and their home, you have to
cross 5 footbridges.
Under each bridge lives a troll and each troll loves
cake!
In order to cross the bridge safely, you must give the
troll half of your cakes.
But the trolls are feeling kind so each troll gives you
back 1 cake.
How many cakes must you start out with to ensure
that you get to your friend's house with 2 cakes - one
cake for each of you?

223. Olivia's birthday is on December 31 yet she always
enjoys a Summer birthday.
Can you explain this?

224. You are standing outside a room and the door is closed. The door has a tight seal surrounding it and no light can escape from the room.
There are three switches outside of the room, numbered 1, 2 and 3 and one of them turns on the light in the room.
You can turn the switches on and off as you wish however you can only open the door to the room once.
If you decide to open the door to the room, then you can't touch any of the switches after this and the game ends.
How do you work out which switch is the one that turns on the light in the room?

225. I'm not a sailor yet a deck's where I'm found
I'm a girl's best friend unless my Queen is around
Call me a trump to make me strong
Will you get this riddle right or wrong?
What am I?

226. What has been around for billions of years yet you get a new one every month?

227. If I get too hot, I simply freeze.
What am I?

228. If you decide to eat me
My owner will eat you
What am I?

229. What tastes better than it smells?

230. The number 854,917,632 is special
     What is special about this?

231. Joe is a spy.
     He wants to send a briefcase containing top secrets
     to another spy, Sam.
     He cannot take the item himself so he employs a
     courier.
     He wants to make sure that the courier does not
     open the briefcase and find out the secrets.
     He has a padlock for the briefcase and a key.
     Sam has a padlock for the briefcase and a key.
     Neither of them has a key for the other one's
     padlock.
     How do they make sure that the secrets stay
     hidden?

232. Dan drives a truck and the truck weighs 2500lbs.
     He comes to a bridge with a warning sign:

     WARNING: WEAK BRIDGE
     NO TRUCKS OVER 2500LBS

     He decides that it is safe to drive over the bridge
     however when he is ¾ of the way across, a small
     bird lands on the roof of the truck.
     Does the bridge break with the added weight of the
     bird?

233. How can you make one disappear?

234. What is grey, like an elephant,
     has a trunk, like an elephant
     and four legs, like an elephant?

235. You love eating eggs for breakfast and decide to buy a rooster so that you can have fresh eggs every day. If you expect to eat 2 eggs a day, how many eggs will you enjoy each week?

236. You return home to find some animals have got into your house. On your bed are 2 dogs, 1 cat and 3 birds.
How many legs are there on the floor?

237. It's 3am. A police patrol see a man lying unconscious with a head injury in front of a store window. The store window is cracked. There's a brick lying next to the man.
The police arrest the man before they take him to hospital.
Why do the police arrest the man?

238. I look flat but I have hidden depths
I can offer food but not shelter
I can be calm but also angry
No one can own me but I contain something every person desires.
What am I?

239. 7 brothers each have birthdays 2 years apart
The youngest brother is 10 years old.
How old is the oldest brother?

240. There is a secret club and to gain entry, you must tell the doorman the password.
The password is different every day
What should you say to the doorman to gain entry?

241. Bill and Ted go camping. It's getting dark and they are cold and hungry.
They need to light a kerosene lamp, a campfire and a portable gas stove.
What should Bill light first?

242. A person is imprisoned in a cell.
The cell has one door, one window high up on the wall, a dirt floor and a shovel.
When the guard comes to check on the prisoner, they find that the prisoner has escaped.
How did he get out of the cell?

243. Two spies have been found out and their enemy has plotted to kill them. They know that the spies take dinner together and enjoy a drink from a shared bottle. The enemy decides to poison the spies.
One spy drinks quickly and survives whilst the other spy sips their drink and dies.
Why did one spy survive if they both poured their drinks from the same bottle?

244. A woman calls the police to state that there has been a break in at her house and her diamonds are missing.
When police arrive, there is a broken window with glass all over the garden and muddy footprints on the carpet inside.
How do the police know that the woman is lying about the break in?

245. You use me from your head to toe
   The harder I work, the smaller I grow
   What am I?

246. I'm a planet and can measure heat and cold
   I'm also a god about which tales are told.
   What am I?

247. Served at a table, I'm small, round and white
   I'm very speedy if you hit me right
   What am I?

248. 6 boys are gathered together in a room.
   There is also a donkey in the room
   The boys have a large stick which they are using to
   beat the donkey.
   Eventually, the donkey falls to the ground.
   The boys are delighted.
   Why?

249. What does not exist but has a name?

250. George came and George went
   Damaged cars, left a dent
   Stole things then threw them aside
   Thank goodness no-one died
   What is George?

251. I can be told, cracked, taken or played
   Heard, seen, loved or made
   What am I?

252. I can build mountains up or reduce them with grind
I can help you to see or turn you blind
What am I?

253. Stare into water and easily see me
But dry as a bone I'll always be
What am I?

254. Round or square, painted or bare
Short or long, to your hands I belong
What am I?

255. I go around in circles but usually straight ahead
I'm found in many places but never on a sled
What am I?

256. There is a field containing 25 sheep.
There is a hole in the fence that surrounds the field.
2 of the sheep escape through the hole.
How many sheep are left in the field?

257. A couple go on vacation for 3 weeks.
They ask their neighbor to check on the house whilst
they are away and deal with any emergencies.
Whilst they are away, there is a power failure which
lasts for 3 days.
When the couple return, the lady's jewelry is
missing but it has not been stolen.
What has happened to the jewels?

258. I have a root but I do not grow
I have a crown but I do not rule
What am I?

259. A thief has been given some information by a security guard. He has drawing of the floorplan of the bank and knows the combination to the safe. The guard has left the door to the room, containing the safe, unlocked.
The thief arrives at night and it is pitch black inside the bank. He has a lighter to see his way.
When he gets to the room with the safe, he realizes it is protected by laser beams linked to an alarm.
How can he see the laser beams so that he can reach the safe?

260. A small explosion then out goes the light
A tickle of pepper makes you loose your sight
What am I?

261. A word you will know, six letters it contains
Remove one letter, now twelve remains
What am I?

262. Even though you might run faster
It becomes harder for you to catch me
What am I?

263. I am shorter than the rest
I often indicate the best
What am I?

264. If you stand on me when people are around watching you might be embarrassed but when standing on me alone you might not like the display I give.
What am I?

265. What word looks the same upside down and in reverse?

266. I am blue, green yellow and red
Spectacular, across the sky spread
Orange, violet, linked to gold
Tricky to find and never to hold
What am I?

267. Where would you be if you can finish a book without finishing a sentence?

268. What I carry would break a man's back
I move slowly on a silver track
What am I?

269. I'm often offered and not accepted and if you use me once, you cannot use me again
What am I?

270. I am with you both night and day
Become irregular, take your breath away
I can take a beating and never bruise
But if I stopped, you would surely loose.
What am I?

271. There is a beautiful expensive yacht in a harbor and on the side of the yacht is a ladder for swimmers. 6ft of the ladder sits above the water line.
The tide comes into the harbor and the water level rises by 2ft.
How much of the ladder will be above the water line now?

272. If you divide 10 by a half and add 7 what is the answer?

273. Ben and his wife lived in a town house. Ben's wife became sick and Ben called the doctor. Ben told the doctor that his wife was ill and he had checked the symptoms online and thought that his wife had appendicitis.
The doctor remembered that he had removed Ben's wife's appendix only 2 years previously so Ben's wife could not have appendicitis.
However, Ben was proved to be correct.
How was it possible that Ben's wife had appendicitis?

274. Sometimes dark and sometimes bright,
I'm seen in the day but mostly at night
Seas and oceans follow my call
Mountains and deserts, not at all
My face is rugged, ancient and gray
But I'm often photographed anyway.
What am I?

275. A grandfather was telling his grandchildren about his bravery at war.
'A live grenade landed close to me and I ran over, picked it up, and threw it back at the enemy.
For my bravery, I was awarded a medal inscribed
Awarded for a Heroic Act in World War I
One of the grandchildren was not impressed and suggested that the story was not true.
What made them think the story was a lie?

276. A detective is working undercover investigating an oil smuggling gang.
The detective goes missing and another detective is sent to the office to investigate.
The people working in the office are named Bob, Bill and Ben.
The detective inspects the undercover officers desk drawers and finds a note reading
710 57735 7718
Who should he arrest?

277. A horse is tied to a rope which is exactly 10 feet long.
The horse is hungry and notices that 15 feet away from the other end of the rope is a juicy bale of hay
How does the horse reach the hay?

278. A nag has a white tail
As the nag moves quickly
The tail becomes shorter
What kind of nag is this?

279. At the beginning of eternity
And the end of space and time
From the start of every ending
And the last of the entire place
What am I?

280. My gleaming fangs and sharp bite
Will bind together on what you write
What am I?

281. Born in an instant with stories to tell
A picture, a sound or even a smell
I might get lost but I'll never die
I can make you smile, laugh or cry
What am I?

282. Can you make two hundred and eighty from forty
seven by adding one letter?

283. Twins each on opposite sides of a beak
Never see each other, not even a peek
What are the twins?

284. A power socket hogs me at one end
Opposite is a spiral with a quirky bend
What am I?

285. Call me nasty, call me quick
You can loose me in a nick
Once you've lost me, others will too
Then a dispute will ensue
What am I?

286. Eight of us travel forwards, not back
Protecting our royals from an enemy attack
What are we?

287. Halo of water, tongue from a tree
I've served man well, historically
Hard to pierce with my skin of stone
Protected Kings and Queens on the throne
What am I?

288. I have no feathers nor wings to fly
But you often spot me in the sky
What am I?

289. I can make you smile, shout or weep
But most of all, you move your feet
What am I?

290. Five tiny things you use each day
One of us is found hay
A cube of ice holds two and three
The fourth is found on a quay
Have you even got a clue?
The last is something inside you
What are we?

291. When I'm a baby, too hot to hold
Quickly cool, can even be cold
I can change with wind and tide
Treasures within me often hide
My form can shelter, offer an abode
Or fall and kill with my heavy load
What am I?

292. A woman normally wears flat shoes but decided
instead to buy a pair of high heels.
She loves the shoes so she wears them to work
where she works as a performer in a stage show.
However, the shoes make her taller than she was
previously which causes her to come to harm as a
result.
What kind of performer is the woman?

293. Every night, before going to sleep, Clare ties a string onto the bedroom door handle.
On the other end of the string is a heavy bell with a loud ring.
Why does she feel this is necessary?

294. Mark is lying on a lounger on a deserted beach.
He's enjoying a 'whodunnit' book.
The sun makes him sleepy so he puts the book down and take a nap.
However, when he wakes the book is gone and he cannot discover the ending of the book.
No-one else has touched the book so where has the book gone?

295. A person is walking home after a dental appointment when they witness a bank robbery.
They phone the police but the person who answers the phone ignores the call and does nothing.
Why?

296. Ella is on a bus and every seat is taken.
An old lady gets on with a walking stick.
Ella offers the lady her seat but the lady refuses to take it and is very embarassed.
Why is this?

297. First I am dry, then I get wet
The longer I swim, the stronger it gets
What am I?

298. Sophia works in a food factory.
   The factory shuts down for a week and Sophie is
   accidentally locked in.
   When she is discovered, Sophia is starving hungry
   having not eaten for a week.
   How is this possible as she is surrounded by food?

299. When you buy me, I am broken, not whole
   Putting me back together is your goal
   I'm exercise for your mind
   As you work, my image you find
   What am I?

300. No feet on me, but I travel afar
   Full of words but no scholar
   No mouth as such but a message I hold
   Carrying news that you need to be told
   What am I?

301. Which is the odd one out?

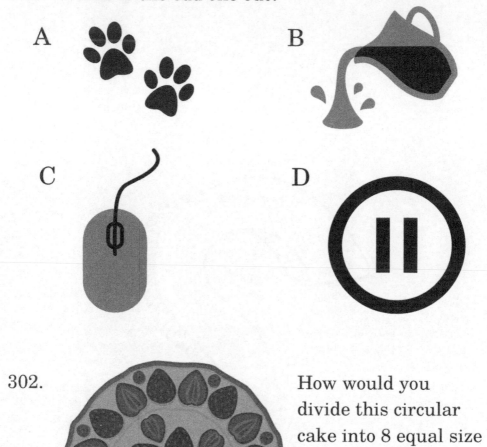

A

B

C

D

302.

How would you divide this circular cake into 8 equal size pieces using only 3 cuts of the knife?

303. What are the next 3 letters in this sequence?

O T T F F S S

304.

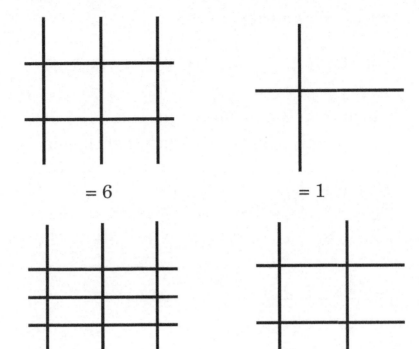

= 6

= 1

= 9

= ??

305. Draw 14 circles below so that there are 7 rows with 4 circles in each row. Each circle can be in more than one row

306. In the following line of letters, cross out six letters to reveal an enjoyable puzzle.

R S I I X D L E D T T L E R E S

307. Alternate full and empty glasses.
You are only allowed to touch 2 of the glasses.

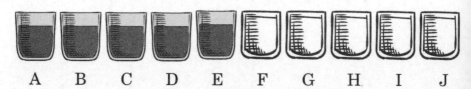

A   B   C   D   E   F   G   H   I   J

308.

can you move 2
of the sticks to
make 7 squares?

309. What game is described here?

P
G
P
G

310. What links these items?

A.   B.   C.

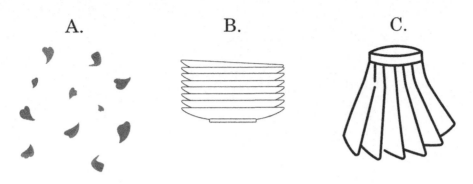

311. Find the dog

312. Which is the odd one out?

A.   B.   C.   D.

313. In the grid below, write six X's in such a way that there is a maximum of one X in each box and there are only two X's in each row and column.

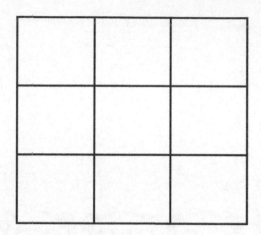

314. Twelve = 6   Six = 3   eight = ?
(the answer is NOT 4)

315.

What comes next in this sequence and why?

A   B   C   D

316. This pair of baseball players are twins.
They are identical in almost every way.
How can you tell them apart when they are playing baseball?

317. What well known saying is depicted here

ITCHE

318. Which fish is the Salmon?

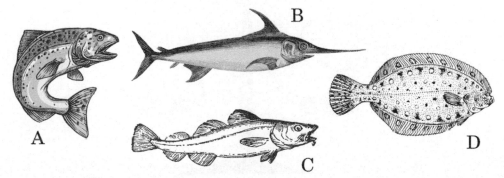

319. Which object is the heaviest?

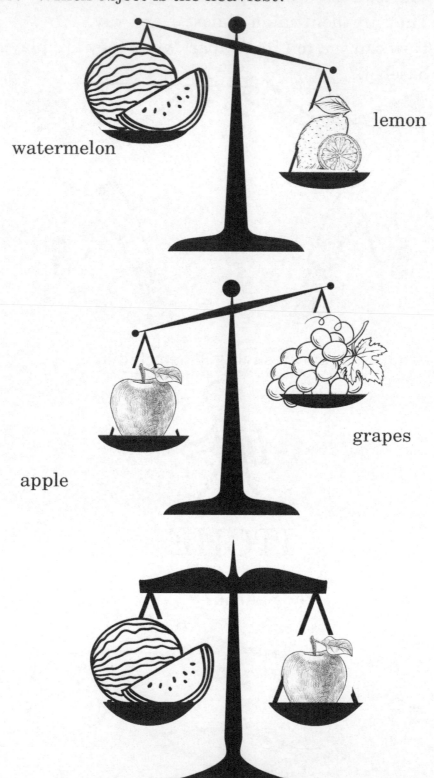

watermelon

lemon

apple

grapes

320. Which candle will burn down first?

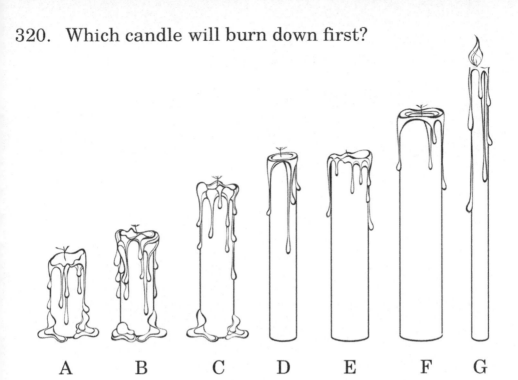

A   B   C   D   E   F   G

321. What well known saying is depicted here

322. Which of these words does not mean 'backwards' in a different language to English?

A. tilbage   D. nyuma
B. achteruit   E. sdrawkcab
C. atgal   F. unazad

323.   Can you find the
         the mistake?

A B C D E F G H I J

324. Which set of letters is the odd one out?

L&S   P&A   H&Y   N&R

325. What well known phrase is depicted here?

1. Games Controller

2. Toilet

3. A burger

4. Money / Coins

5. A one story house does not have stairs.

6. Trouble

7. Alphabet

8. He was bald and had no hair on his head.

9. Crack me - I'm an egg

10. All of them have 28 days although some have more!

11. A computer mouse

12. FOX - OX - X (Roman numeral for 10)

13. Paid work

14. A coat of paint

15. Your name

16. The Nile. It just hadn't been discovered yet!

17. Your age

18. Money

19. A Door

20. A Ruler

21. A Pillow

22. Counterfeit money

23. Day and Night

24. The North Pole

25. The King, Queen and Twins are all beds.

26. Seven: S - even

27. February as there are less days in this month than any other month.

28. A needle

29. A metal staple

30. A cobweb

31. Silence

32. Light

33. A mirror

34. The river was frozen over

35. Dry rocks

36. Birthday cake candles

37. A computer

38. As many as you want - you can sleep at night.

39. The book is written in braille.

40. School

41. An envelope

42. A comb

43. Each sailor has their back to the side of the ship and they are looking across the ship.

44. They are triplets

45. Honey (take away the H and Y)

46. A dentist

47. A honey bee

48. A banana

49. A rose

50. A salt shaker

51. A mug of coffee

52. A river

53. A promise

54. The person has hiccups and the barista makes him better by scaring him.

55. A telephone

56. The person accidentally stabbed themselves with an icicle which has now melted into a pool of water.

57. Your breath

58. A razor for shaving

59. They jumped out of the plane but their parachute failed to open.

60. They called the person in the next room using the hotel phone to dial the room number. The person in the next room was snoring and the phone call wakes them up.

61. A banknote

62. An echo

63. The diner had added ground pepper to the soup and could still see the pepper floating on the top of the replacement soup.

64. Romance

65. A piano

66. Stars in the sky

67. The door to the cell is unlocked

68. All animals that can jump - Cars can't jump

69. They are in Iceland in December and by 4pm, the sun has already set at this time of year and at this latitude so the person does not have a shadow.

70. Agreed - A greed

71. An ice cube

72. She was his sister

73. James is a cat and Lisa is a fish and lived in a fishtank hence the pool of water on the floor

74. The letter E

75. Toothbrush

76. A windmill

77. A deck of cards

78. Money

79. The robbery is happening on a television drama they are watching

80. The motorist has changed the tire for the spare and the flat tire is not on the wheel of the car

81. They fell off the bottom step of the ladder

82. Sleep

83. Your reflection

84. A tree

85. The letter 'T'

86. A thorn in my shoe

87. A window

88. A toothbrush

89. Music

90. Skin

91. A glove

92. A kiss

93. The clocks when back an hour whilst the person was out.

94. Four - Three spelling mistakes and the mistaken claim that the sentence contains only two mistakes

95. History

96. A book

97. A mirror

98. A bottle

99. *Opportunity*

100. *A shadow*

101. *John was appearing as an actor in a play at the theatre*

102. *It is a game of chess and the knight has taken the bishop*

103. *Pizza*

104. *The wife is a stunt person and has been working on a movie set*

105. *The hospital has cured the person of deafness and knew that this was the case when he heard the phone ringing*

106. *A golf ball*

107. *A choice*

108. *A freezer*

109. *Tom*

110. *A sponge*

111. *Your future*

112. *Nine*

113. *An anchor*

114. *A cloud*

115. *Rain*

116. *A well*

117. *Are you asleep yet?*

118. *They drifted off course in separate directions so that when they landed they were 1 hour walk apart with the drop zone lying between them.*

119. *The person in the house is a burglar. There is a parrot in the house who has spoken the phrase 'Stick 'Em Up!' and the burglar thinks this is someone with a gun. However, they swiftly realise it is the parrot which makes them laugh and they leave the house.*

120. *Water*

121. *The letter 'R'*

122. *A Tree*

123. *Because when you have found it, you stop looking for it.*

124. *A keyboard*

125. *Your tongue*

126. *A bed*

127. *A broom*

128. *The plane was on the ground at the time of the fire and it was a small plane so the exit was not far from the ground and therefore easily jumped.*

129. *A baby elephant*

130. *Scent, Cent and Sent*

131. *Charcoal*

132. *A Tree*

133. *A Pencil*

134. *A Skateboard*

135. *An onion*

136. *An iceberg*

137. *Love*

138. *A snowflake*

139. *A plant*

140. *Your word*

141. *A needle*

142. *Noise*

143. *Legs*

144. *Yesterday, Today and Tomorrow*

145. *A watermelon*

146. *Plates*

147. *I am a religious nun*

148. *A hat*

149. *Time*

150. *Bones in the ear. The smallest bones in the human body are named the hammer and the anvil.*

151. *Penguins live a the South Pole and polar bears at the North Pole*

152. *0*

153. *His birthday is on December 31. Today is January 1, so he celebrates his next birthday at the end of this year.*

154. *Your mind*

155. Max was born at 11:55pm on February 28th
Mim was born at 12:05am on February 29th son only
celebrates her birthday when it is a leap year.

156. The gardener. As it was Christmas, it must have
been December and grass does not grow nor need
cutting in December.

157. The letter 'R'
It is the 3rd letter of March, the 8th letter of
November, the 9th letter of September and the 7th
letter of October.

158. A magnet

159. Stop imagining that you are in the room!

160. Zebra

161. The wind

162. A car which has a horsepower, a catalytic converter
and a trunk for luggage.

163. On a clock eg 9am plus 5 hours takes you to 2pm.

164. A ring donut

165. An apology

166. The person shooting them is a photographer and they
are using a camera and not a gun.

167. A hole.

168. 5 minutes - they are all in the same pan of water.

169. Arms (it is an anagram)

170. Andrew

171. Post Office

172. The Ocean

173. Heroine - He, Her, Hero, Heroine

174. Adding the letters 'ng'

175. Weighty - Eighty - Eight

176. Chicago

177. What are <u>you</u> wearing? You are driving the bus!

178. Everyone in the car is married therefore the driver is not single.

179. You throw the ball into the air and gravity brings the ball back down to return it to you.

180. A doorbell

181. A basketball hoop

182. The seal of the envelope was laced with poison and when the man licked the seal, he was poisoned and died.

183. A door lock

184. The number 8
    Chopped in half becomes 0
    On it's side becomes the infinity symbol ∞

185. 777-77=700

186. I am a wake up alarm

187. 4 eggs - you ate the 2 that you broke

188. *Only one of the six people is a man - all the rest are women.*

189. *3 - One cat, one dog and one rabbit*

190. *They should pick the second dentist.*
As there are only 2 dentists in the town, they must look after each other's teeth.
Thus the second dentist, with the bad teeth, must look after the first dentist with the good teeth.

191. *Stable - Table - Able - Stable*

192. *3 coffees as the grandmother is also a mother and the mother is also a daughter so there were 3 people present.*

193. *Tom simply writes the words 'Jim's exact weight' on the paper.*

194. *They are an astronaut and are doing a space walk when the hole is torn in their uniform.*

195. *Stone - take away 'one' and you are left with 'st' which is an abbreviation for stone.*

196. *Your father.*

197. *A hole.*

198. *The bus driver was walking, not driving a bus.*

199. *The sun*

200. *A guitar*

201. *What would you say **I if** told you there was a mistake in this sentence? Do you know what the mistake is?*

202. A beehive

203. You are on a merry-go-round

204. A paper plane

205. A clock

206. Coconut trees grow coconuts and do not have bananas!

207. Alex must be the person who is playing chess with Lucy.

208. The youngest person is the baby of the pregnant lady.

209. Own lea too <u>words</u> our rite inn <u>this</u> sentance.
    Witch too our rite?
    (Only two words are right in this sentence.
    Which two are right?)

210. Bookkeeper

211. Sam is the murderer.
    The numbers in the clue indicate the months of the year and the first letter of each month indicated spell out Sam's name:
    9 = September = S
    4 = April = A
    3 = March = M

212. Seventy Seven

213. The prisoner waits until the sun sets and the magnifying glass room is in darkness when it is safe for him to enter.

214. *A bubble*

215. *One of the sons is also a father making three people in total - a grandfather, a father and a son. The grandfather is a father to the father.*

216. *Bee*

217. *A decimal point making 5.7*

218. *You do not knock on your own hotel door.*

219. *They are all telling the truth as the doctor, lawyer and teacher are all John's sisters.*

220. *A zip.*

221. *Lucy sings 'Happy Birthday' to Bartholomew.*

222. *You need to start out with 2 cakes.*
    At each bridge, you give the troll half of the cakes - 1 cake.
    They give you back 1 cake so you still have 2 cakes after each bridge.

223. *Olivia lives in the Southern Hemisphere where December is a Summer month.*

224. *You turn on the first switch for 5 minutes.*
    You turn off the first switch and quickly turn on the second switch.
    You open the door to the room.
    If the light is on, the correct switch is switch 2.
    If the light is off, touch the bulb. If it is warm then the correct switch is switch 1.
    If it is cold, the correct switch is switch 3.

225. *The King of Diamonds in a deck of cards*

226. *The moon*

227. *A computer*

228. *A fish hook*

229. *Your tongue*

230. *The digits 1-9 are in alphabetical order*

231. *Joe locks the case using his padlock.*
When the case arrives at Sam's, he adds his padlock and sends the courier with the case back to Joe.
Joe removes his padlock using his key and sends the courier with the case back to Sam.
Sam can now open the case with his key as only his own padlock is on the case.

232. *The bridge is safe because the truck has used fuel to cross the bridge and the weight of the bird is less than the weight of the fuel that has been consumed so the truck still weighs 2500lbs*

233. *Add a 'g' and it's gone!*

234. *A picture of an elephant*

235. *Sadly, you will not enjoy any eggs as roosters don't lay eggs, only hens lay eggs.*

236. *There are 6 legs on the floor. 4 legs belonging to the bed and your legs.*
All the animals are on the bed and thus their legs are not on the floor.

237. The man is trying to rob the store. He has thrown the brick at the window and cracked it and the brick has bounced back and hit him on the head causing injury.

238. The ocean

239. 22 years old

240. You should say 'different' as this is the password

241. Bill should light a match

242. The prisoner dug the dirt floor and made a pile of dirt under the window so that they could reach the window and climb out to freedom.

243. The poison was not in the drink but it was in the ice in the glass. The spy who drank quickly finished their drink before the ice melted and were not poisoned whereas the one who sipped their drink gave the ice time to melt and subsequently was poisoned and died.

244. Glass in the garden means that the window was broken from the inside of the house and thus the break in has been staged in order to claim the insurance money for the diamonds.

245. A bar of soap

246. Mercury

247. A ping pong ball

248. The donkey is a pinata

249. *Nothing*

250. *George is a hurricane*

251. *I am a joke*

252. *Sand - sand in the form of glass helps us to see*

253. *A reflection*

254. *Fingernails*

255. *A wheel*

256. *A trick question - sorry! There won't be any sheep left in the field as they will follow the first two through the hole and all the sheep will escape.*

257. *The lady hid her jewelry in a bag in the freezer.*
The power failure caused all the food in the freezer to melt and be inedible.
The neighbor wanted to be helpful and threw away the contents of the freezer.

258. *A tooth*

259. *He uses the lighter to set light to the floorplan drawing thus creating smoke which then allows him to see the laser beams.*

260. *A sneeze*

261. *Dozens - remove one letter to get 'dozen'*

262. *Your breath*

263. *Your thumb*

264. *Weighing scales*

265. *SWIMS*

266. *A rainbow*

267. *You would be in prison*

268. *A snail*

269. *An excuse*

270. *Your heart*

271. *There will still be 6ft of the ladder above the water line as the yacht will rise as the tide comes in.*

272. *27 since 10 DIVIDED by a ½ = 20,   20 + 7 = 27*

273. *Ben had divorced his first wife and remarried in the 2 years that had elapsed since his first wife had her appendix out.*

274. *The moon*

275. *The words 'World War I' could not have been inscribed on the medal since the Second World War had not started and no-one expected it to happen.*

276. *When viewed upside down, the note reads 'Bill Sells Oil' so he should arrest Bill*

277. *The horse can easily walk over to the hay since the rope that the horse is tied to is not tied to anything else at the other end.*

278. *The nag is a threaded needle*

279. *The letter 'e'*

280. *A staple*

281. *Memories*

282. *Forty x seven makes two hundred and eighty*
    $40 \times 7 = 280$

283. *Eyes*

284. *A pig*

285. *Temper*

286. *Pawns in a game of chess*

287. *A castle*
    The halo of water is the moat and the wooden tongue is the drawbridge

288. *A helicopter*

289. *Music*

290. *Vowels*
    Five tiny things you use each day
    *One of us is found h*a*y*
    A cube of i*ce holds two and three*
    *The fourth is found on a q*ua*y*
    Have you even got a clue?
    *The last is something inside y*o*u*

291. *Rock*

292. *The woman is an assistant to a knife thrower.*
    When she stands at the target in her high heels, she appears taller than she did previously and the knife thrower misjudges the throw and harms her.

293. *Clare is a sleepwalker. If she tries to leave the bedroom in her sleep, the noise from the bell will wake her husband so that he can guide her back to bed.*

294. *The tide came in and the waves took the book to sea. Mark did not notice the tide since his lounger raised him above the shallow waters.*

295. *The person's mouth is numb from the dental treatment and they are talking gibberish. The call handler thinks they are drunk and ignores the call.*

296. *Ella is only 4 years old and she is sitting on her Dad's lap.*

297. *A teabag*

298. *The factory is a canning factory. All the food is in cans rather than waiting to be canned as the factory is closing down for a week. Sophia cannot open any of the cans as she does not have a can opener.*

299. *A jigsaw puzzle*

300. *A letter*

301. *C is the odd one out as it is a computer mouse.*
The others are all variations on the same sounding word:
A Paws, B Pours, C Pause.

302.

Make the first 2 cuts as shown then the third cut is a horizonal cut through the middle of the cake

303. *E N T*
They are the inital letters of the words used when writing the numbers One to Ten:
One, Two, Three, Four, Five, Six, Seven, Eight, Nine, Ten

304. *4*
The answer is the number of times the lines intersect.

305.

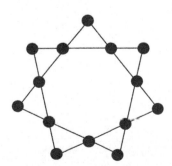

306. Cross out the *SIX LETTERS* to reveal the word *RIDDLE*

307. <u>Pour</u> *the liquid from glass B to glass G and glass D to glass I*

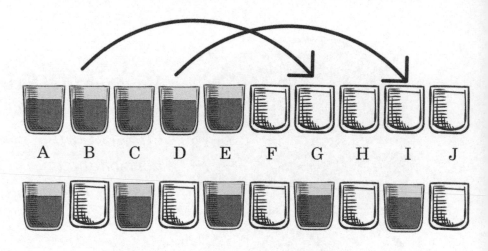

308.

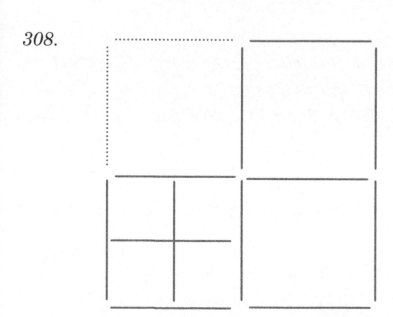

309. *Ping Pong - P* <u>in</u> *G and P* <u>on</u> *G*

310. *The items are all anagrams of each other:*
PETALS   PLATES   PLEATS

311.

312. *C is the odd one out as it is a left hand and the others
are all right hands.*

313.

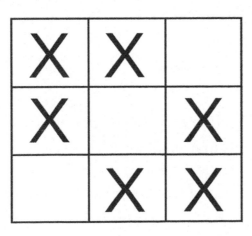

313. *The answer is 5 - the number of letters in each word.*

315. *B - they are all pairs of numbers with the second number being a reflection of the first*

1Ʇ 2ꙅ 3Ɛ 4ᴚ

316. *One is left handed and one is right handed so they have a different hand at the base of the bat.*

317. *Walking on thin ice*
(A person walking on 'TH' in 'ICE' letters)

318. *A is the salmon*
B is swordfish
C is cod and
D is plaice

319. *Lemon > Watermelon*
Apple > Grapes
Apple = Watermelon
Thus
Lemon > Watermelon or Apple > Grapes
Lemon is the heaviest

320. *G will burn down first since it is the only candle that is lit.*

321. *Hole in one.*

322. E as 'sdrawkcab' is 'backwards' written backwards.

323.   Can you find (the)
            (the) mistake?

A B C D E F G H I J

324. N&R are the odd ones out as the other pairs of letters
     make a word if you replace the '&' with the letters
     'and'

     LandS, PandA, HandY but NandR is not a word

325. See you around

Other books by Alex Smart

Available on Amazon

About the author

Alex Smart has two adult 'kids' and lives in a small village in Devon, England with her patient husband.

She enjoys spending quality time with friends and family and likes to inject amusing games and quizzes into any social gathering.

Alex also enjoys making people smile with a gently mocking greeting card or novelty gift.

She created these books to be a fun and inexpensive gift for the 'hard to buy for' people in life.

"I love giving people fun gifts that make them laugh! "

Keep in touch and enjoy some exclusive freebies at the website
www.thingstodowhileyoupoo.com

Printed in Great Britain
by Amazon

31198930R00050